Card AND Dice Games AND Tricks

MUD PUDDLE BOOKS, INC.
New York, New York

Published by
Mud Puddle Books, Inc.
54 W. 21st Street
Suite 601
New York, NY 10010 USA

info@mudpuddlebooks.com

HB
HINKLER
BOOKS

Hinkler Books Pty Ltd
17 – 23 Redwood Drive
Dingley Victoria 3172 Australia
www.hinklerbooks.com

© Hinkler Books Pty Ltd 2004

Written by: Graeme Johnstone
Edited by: Heather Hammonds
Design: JM Artworks (Aust) Pty Ltd

ISBN: 1 59412 044 7

Printed and bound in China.

Contents

Introduction

Welcome To The wonderful world of cards and dice!

With a pack of cards or some dice, life will always be enjoyable. You can intrigue, amaze and amuse family and friends, or an even bigger audience, with card tricks. Or you can have hours of fun playing card or dice games.

We have selected the best card games and tricks, and dice games, for your enjoyment. You will find games in this book that can be played by one, two, three, four, or as many players as you like.

The top card game, Whist, is well worth learning. Not only is it a lot of fun, it is also the basis of much bigger games such as Five Hundred and Solo, which you can learn later.

When performing card tricks, you need to be able to convince your audience with a nice line of "patter", or clever talk. Above all, you need to practice, practice, practice.
Then before you know it, you'll be a great card magician!

We also recommend that you take the time to learn the dice game of Craps. Craps is a very popular dice game, played in casinos around the world. It can also be enjoyed at home, among friends and family.

So let's begin having fun with cards and dice!

10 Things You Should Know About Cards

1. There are 52 cards in a pack.

2. The 52 cards are divided into four groups of 13 cards each.

3. These groups of 13 are usually known as "suits."

4. There are four suits – two black suits and two red suits.

5. The four suits are the Clubs, Spades, Hearts and Diamonds.

6. The Clubs and Spades are the black suits, and the Hearts and Diamonds are the red suits.

7. The 13 cards usually go in this order: Ace, 2, 3, 4, 5, 6, 7, 8, 9, 10, Jack, Queen, King.

8. In some games, the Ace is made the highest card, even higher than the King.

9. There are also two Jokers in each pack, but these are used only in certain games.

10. When the Joker is used in a game, its value varies according to the game and its rules – it may be a Wild Card, or the highest card, or the lowest card.

Shuffling & Dealing

Shuffling

There are various methods of shuffling cards and with practice, you will be able to do them all. The most basic shuffle to begin with is the Overhand Shuffle.

1. Hold the pack of cards with the thumb and fingers of your right hand.

2. Bring both your hands together.

3. Use your left thumb to take cards from the top of the pack, pulling off a block of several cards at once.

4. Leave the remainder of the pack in your right hand.

5. Separate your hands completely.

6. Hold the block of cards in your left hand between your thumb and fingers.

7. Lift your left thumb, just enough to allow the bundle of cards in your right hand to be inserted at various points, into the pack sitting in your left hand.

8. Begin to shuffle, and continue until you have mixed the cards together.

Dealing

Dealing is the term for removing the cards from the pack, either one by one or as a group. To deal the cards, hold the pack in your left hand and use your thumb to push cards off the top of the pack. Use your right hand to draw the cards up, and distribute them.

CARD GAMES

Here are some of the best card games around! Play them with family and friends, for hours of fun!

Beggar My Neighbor

This is a nice simple game but it can get very exciting, as people have to pay up, or collect debts. The winner is the person who ends up with all the cards.

1. Take a deck of cards, take out the Jokers, and deal the 52 cards evenly to all players.

2. The first player turns up his/her top card, and places it face-up on the table. Then the next player turns his/her first card up and the game proceeds around the table, everyone taking a turn.

3. If a card that is turned up is a numbered card, from 2 to 9, then the game continues. But when a card is a picture card or an Ace, it means that the next player in line has to "pay". If it is a Jack, he/she has to "pay" one card. If it is a Queen, it is two cards. If it is a King, it is three cards and if it is an Ace, four cards. All cards are paid out on the one pile in the middle of the table.

4. If the "debt" is completed with a numbered card, the player who turned up the picture card or Ace has to take the pile on the table, turn it face-down, include it with his/her playing hand and the game continues. If, however, a picture card or Ace turns up during the payout, then the "debt" is wiped out and the next player in line has to start paying out.

5. Keep going like this until one player holds all cards and you have a winner.

TIP! Of the picture cards, the Jack is the best to have, because you only have to "pay" out one.

Bingo

This is like Bingo, the old game played in halls where numbers are called out and players mark them off a sheet. But instead it is played with cards. It is a great party game for three, four or five players, plus a caller. The winner of each game wins a prize, so it is a good idea to have little treats or candy as rewards.

It is lots of fun!

1. The caller takes the Jokers out of the deck, shuffles the cards, and deals five cards to each player.

2. Players place their cards face-up in front of themselves.

3. The caller goes through the pack, one at a time, and calls out the face value of each card as it comes up.

4. A player who has a card the same value as the one called, turns it face-down.

5. The first person to have all cards turned face-down calls "Bingo!" and wins the round. And a prize!

TIP! Keep an eye on your cards, listen carefully, and concentrate, rather than gazing at the candy!

Chase That Ace!

Lots of players can be in this game. If you use candy as counters, they winner will get to eat them!

1. Each player starts with three counters. You can use coins or matches, but the best idea is to get Mom to let you use candy.

2. The idea is not to end up with the lowest card. Clubs are the lowest suit of all, followed by Diamonds, Hearts, then Spades. The Ace is the lowest card and the King is the highest.

3. Each person puts one counter in. Then the dealer deals out one card to each person, face-down. No one is allowed to look at the card.

4. The remaining cards are left in a pile, face-down.

5. The player on the dealer's left goes first, looking at the card he/she holds. If it is a King, he/she turns it face-up and places it on the table.

6. If it is anything else, he/she has two choices – either say "Stand" and hold the card, or exchange it with the card of the player on his or her left.

7. The next player does the same, and the game continues around the table until it reaches the dealer. The dealer can either declare a King, or "Stand". But if the dealer wants to exchange, they cannot do so with the player on their left. The dealer exchanges their card for the top card of the remaining pack.

8. All cards are turned face-up, and whoever holds the lowest puts a counter into the kitty.

9. The player at the dealer's left gathers the cards and places them at the bottom of the pack, and deals a new hand.

10. When a player's third counter goes into the kitty, he/she is out, and the hands continue until there is one survivor.

11. If you have used candy as counters, this is the time when the lucky winner gets to eat the lot!

TIP! Keep an eye out for those low cards and try to get rid of them - they can cause big problems!

Cheat

Normally, you are not supposed to cheat in this world. But, hey, what the heck... just for once, in this game, you can! If you use candy as counters, the winner will get to eat them!

1. The dealer deals the cards to all players, until all the cards are dealt.

2. The player to the left of the dealer goes first, placing one card face-down on the table and naming the card's value. For example, "Six."

3. The idea of the game is to continue the cards in numbered order. So the next player puts a card face-down on top of the first card and calls, "Seven."

4. Then the next player puts a card face-down on top of the pile and says, "Eight."

5. It keeps going like this until it reaches King, and then you start at Ace. But here's the cheating bit. You might not have an Eight, so you put any card down and say "Eight" anyway! The skill is to get away with it.

6. If a player thinks another player is cheating, then he/she can challenge that player. If the challenged player is caught out cheating, then he/she has to pick up the whole pile of cards. But if the challenged player is telling the truth, then the challenger has to take up the cards.

7. The player who picked up the cards puts a card down and nominates it, to start the next round.

8. The player who gets rid of all their cards is the winner. And the best cheat!

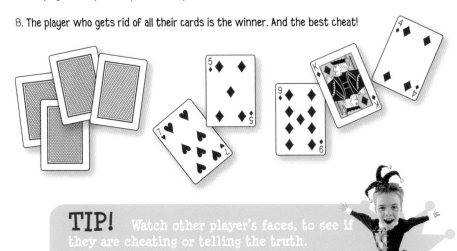

TIP! Watch other player's faces, to see if they are cheating or telling the truth. And if you really want to be a super-cheat, place two or even three cards down when it's your turn, as if they were one!

CLock PaTience

Tick-tock, tick-tock, this game is for one player, is very easy to learn, and is a whole lot of fun on a rainy afternoon!

1. You need one pack of cards and plenty of elbow room.

2. Take out the Jokers, set them aside and shuffle the pack very well.

3. Now imagine a big clock in front of you, on the table. Place one card, face-down, at arm's length away from you. This card is the twelve o'clock position.

4. Place a card, face-down, next to it. But angle it so that it is starting to make a circle. This card is at one o'clock.

5. Now do a card at two o'clock, three o'clock and so on.

6. When you have reached eleven o'clock, put the next card in the middle of the circle.

7. Start again at twelve o'clock, work your way around, and again, when you have reached eleven o'clock, put a card in the middle.

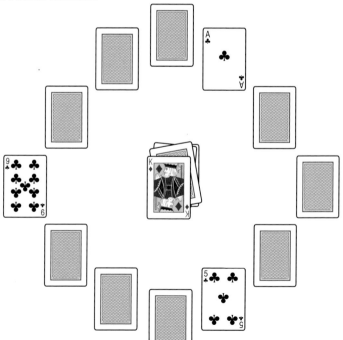

8. Eventually you will have twelve piles of four cards forming a clock face, and the thirteenth pile of four cards in the middle.

9. Now take the top card off the pile in the middle and turn it face-up. If it is, say, a Three, then put it face-up at the bottom of the pile, at three o'clock. If it is a Six, then it goes under the pile at six o'clock, and so on. Jacks are at eleven o'clock, Queens at twelve and the King goes under the pile in the middle.

10. Now turn up the top card of whichever pile you placed the first card under. Say this is a Seven. It goes under the pile at seven o'clock, and you turn up the top card on that one. And so on.

11. Keep going like this for as long as you can.

12. The idea is to fill out the clock dial before the last King is turned up.

Concentration

This is a mind game which is easy to play, but requires a good memory and the ability to concentrate. Usually it is played by two people, but you can play with more if you like.

1. Take out the Jokers and shuffle the pack. Then lay all 52 cards face-down on the table. You can either lay them in rows and columns, which is the easier game, or spread them out randomly, which is more difficult.

2. The first player turns one card – a card from anywhere on the table – face-up, and then turns a second card face-up from anywhere on the table.

3. The player looks at the cards. If they are a matching pair, he/she picks them up and puts them aside in his/her pile.

4. If the cards are not a matching pair, the player turns them face-down, leaving them back on the table where they were.

5. Now the second player turns up two cards. Again, if they are a matching pair he/she takes them. If not, they are turned face-down and put back where they were.

6. The players continue to take turns, turning over two cards at a time.

7. When all cards have been turned over and collected, each player counts up how many he or she has, and the person with the most pairs wins.

TIP! Look at each card carefully when it is turned over, and try to memorize its spot, so that when you next pick up its "pair", you will know immediately where to look.

Dominos

This is a variation of the game of Dominos. But in this case, you line up the cards in sequence, starting with a number Seven. It is a game for two or more players.

1. Take out the Jokers and shuffle the pack. Then deal the cards one at a time to each player, until all cards are dealt. If some players get one more card than others, don't worry. It will even out when the play begins.

2. The player to the left of the dealer begins. He or she needs a Seven to open. If not, that player misses a turn and knocks on the table to "Pass". The first player to put down a Seven begins the game.

3. Each player now takes turns to build on the Seven and the other cards, as they are put down. If a player can't go, they knock.

4. The Seven can be built on in several ways. Say it is a Seven of Hearts. A player can place a Six of Hearts to the left of it, or an Eight of Hearts to the right. Or the player can place a Seven of a different suit above or below it.

5. Players continue to take turns and build on the row of cards, knocking when they cannot go. Ultimately, you will find the four suits end up in four rows, one above the other.

The player who uses all their cards first is the winner!

TIP! This can become a game of strategy when you play the cards to your advantage. One technique is to hold onto cards that you can play later.

Donkey

This is another good game to play with candy as counters!

1. Put one less counter in the middle of the table than there are players. If there are four playing, put three counters in.

2. From the pack, take out as many sets of four cards as there are players. So, for four people, take out the four Aces, the four Twos, the four Threes and the four Fours. Put the rest aside.

3. Shuffle the sixteen cards and deal them out, four cards to each player. The aim is to be the first player to collect a set of four matching cards.

4. Each player looks at their cards and works out what to keep, and what to give away.

5. The dealer calls "Pass" and right away, each player passes a card, face-down, to the player on their left.

6. As soon as all players have looked at their cards, the dealer calls "Pass" again, and again all players pass a card, face-down, to the player on their left.

7. Remember, you cannot look at the card you are receiving until you have passed your card on.

8. When a player collects a set of four, he/she places them down and picks up a counter.

9. The last player is left with nothing, and is the Donkey!

TIP! Avoid playing this game with a brand new pack - between you and the candy, the cards will get very sticky!

Elevens

This is an easy version of the game Patience, but it still tests your concentration and is great fun when you get the game out.

1. Take out the Jokers and shuffle the pack. Then deal out nine cards, laying them face-up in three rows of three cards.

2. Take the remainder of the pack in your hand. The aim is to use the cards to cover the cards on the table that add up to eleven.

3. In this game, the Ace is worth one, picture cards are worth ten, and all other cards are face value. So, if a Nine and a Two are visible, they make eleven. So you place the first card from the pack face-up on one of them, and the next one on the other. Same goes for any combination of cards that make eleven.

4. You can also cover a Jack, Queen and King if those three are all face-up at the one time.

5. Continue until there are no more combinations of eleven on the table. You win if you use all the cards in the pack!

TIP! Sometimes, it's good to play this game when you've already played another, harder form of Patience and just need a little taste of success before you go back to it.

15

Fish

Fish is often the first card game that anybody learns. You can play with anything up to six players. It is simple, fun and a great game to play with younger cousins at family gatherings. The aunties will be very impressed.

1. Take out the Jokers and shuffle the pack.

2. The dealer deals eight cards to each person, one at a time, starting, as usual, from the left. The remainder of the pack is placed face-down on the table.

3. Each person looks at his/her cards and matches any pairs, taking them out and putting them face-down on the table in front of them.

4. The idea of the game is to ask the player on your right for cards that will match with yours, and make up pairs.

5. The game begins with the person on the right of the dealer. This player turns to the person on his/her right and asks, "Do you have a ------?" (naming the card in his/her hand that he/she wishes to make into a pair).

6. The other player has two choices. If he/she has the requested card, they answer "Yes" and hand over the card to the player who asked for it, who then makes up the pair and puts it face-down on the table.

7. If the other player does not have the card, the reply is "Fish", in which case, the person who made the request goes "fishing". That is, they take the top card from the face-down pack on the table and add it to their hand.

8. If the "Fish" card makes a pair with one of the cards in the player's hand, then the pair can be put down on the table with the player's other pairs.

9. If the "Fish" card does not match any of the player's cards, then the player has to add it to his/her hand.

10. Now it is the next player's turn to ask for a card from the person to his/her right.

11. Continue this with each player taking a turn.

12. When a person has matched all of the cards in his/her hand, he/she takes eight more from the deck and continues as before.

13. When there are no cards left to match, the person with the most pairs of cards, wins the game.

TIP
Watch the expressions on the player's faces when they pick cards up and put pairs down, to try and work out what they are aiming for and whether they might have something you need.

Variation
Agree before you start the game that, instead of the player whose turn it is having to ask the person to his/her right, he/she can ask anybody who is taking part in the game.

Fun
For really little kids, attach a metal paper clip to each card and lay all the cards face-down and separately on the table. Attach a magnet on a string to a ruler and then, instead of picking up from the upturned pack, "go fishing".
Even big kids love to do this!

German Whist

This game is played in a similar way to Whist, but it is easier to play and good practice for other Whist-type games. Unlike Whist, which needs four players, this is a great game for two players.

1. Remove the Jokers from a pack of cards, and then cut the pack for the deal. This means that one player picks up part of the pack and the other takes the top card from the remaining pile and turns it face-up, to see what it is. In this case, the lowest card takes the deal. Ace is the lowest card in this game.

2. Deal alternative cards until each player has thirteen cards. Place the rest of the pack face-down on the table and turn the top card face-up. The suit on this card is "trumps", or the leading suit, for the first game. This means that cards of this suit will always beat cards of any other suit. The only card that will beat a trump card is a higher card of the same suit.

3. The other player leads, and the dealer must follow suit if he/she can. If he/she cannot follow suit, they may either play another card, or trump. Remember, a trump card, no matter how small, beats a card of any other suit.

4. Two cards have been played and the winner of the "trick" (round) puts them to one side (they have no bearing on the game). He/she then takes the exposed card from the top of the pack and adds it to his/her hand.

5. The loser takes the next card from the pack without showing its face, and adds it to his/her hand. The aim is to build up a good hand for a final show-down. He/she then turns the next card face-up on the top of the pack.

6. The winner leads, and so play goes on until all the face-down pile has gone.

7. Then the final battle begins. The aim is to win as many tricks as you can with the hand of thirteen cards that you have built up.

8. Winner of the last trick leads.

9. The winner of the game is the person who takes seven or more tricks.

10. To work out how many points you have earned in each game, subtract six from the number of tricks you have taken. For example, if you have taken nine tricks, 9 – 6 = 3, therefore, your score for that round is 3. If you took ten tricks you score 4 points, and so on. Your opponent scores 0. At the end of the game , the highest score wins.

Jane	Mary
9 tricks	10 tricks
9-6=3	10-6=4

TIP! The face-up card on the top of the pack is important. If you don't need it, you may even try NOT to win the point. Remember, the card underneath may be a good one!

Gin Rummy

There are endless variations of this game and it is important that all players are aware of the rules that you are adopting, before the start of the game. Any number from two upwards can play. If Jokers are used, they are wild – that is, they can be used as a substitute for any card in the pack. Two packs of cards may be shuffled together and used.

1. Cut the pack for the deal, as in Step 1 in German Whist. The player who cuts the lowest, deals. Ace is low. The deal goes in turn, to the left.

2. Dealer deals seven cards to each player. They may be singly, or in three twos and a one.

3. Left over cards are placed face-down in the middle. The top card is turned up and placed beside the stack.

4. The aim is to collect sets of three or more cards of the same value (for example, three Queens or four Sevens), or sequences of cards of the same suit (2, 3, 4 of Diamonds; Ten, Jack, Queen of Spades).

5. When all seven cards in your hand are comprised of sets or sequences, then you have a Gin Rummy, and you can go out. You can tally the cards in your hand (10 points for a picture card, 5 points for a number card), take a bonus of 20 for going out, and add it to your score.

6. All other players must tally the cards in their hands (10 points for a picture card, 5 points for a number card) and take it off his/her score.

7. The person with the highest score at the end of the game wins.

TIP! This game can be varied in many ways, and no two groups play it exactly the same way. It is a lead-up to Canasta, which is its more complicated form.

OLd Maid

This is a great game, the idea being not to end up with the Old Maid – the Queen of Spades!

1. Take a Queen of Clubs from the pack and put it aside. Then deal the remaining fifty-one cards out to all players. If there are three of you they will go evenly, but if not, don't worry.

2. Each player then looks at his/her cards, and looks for pairs. They place any pairs they have face-down on the table.

3. Each player then collects his/her remaining cards and fans them out.

4. Each player then offers the fanned-out cards to the player on his/her left, facing the cards away so the other player can't see what the cards are.

5. The neighbor takes one card. If the card pairs with one of his/her cards, he/she puts it down on the table. If not, he/she has to keep it in his/her hand.

6. Again, the cards are offered to the player on the left, and any pairs are placed down on the table.

7. Keep going like this until the last pair goes down. There will be one card left, and the person holding it is left with the Old Maid!

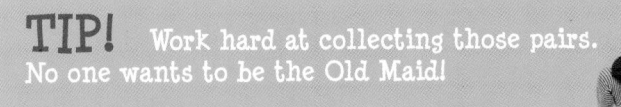

TIP! Work hard at collecting those pairs. No one wants to be the Old Maid!

Pairs

This is a variation of the game Elevens, and is also an easy Patience game to get out.

1. Take a pack, take out the Jokers, and deal three rows of three cards, face-up.

2. Whenever you see two cards of the same value, pick them up and put them to one side, filling in their spaces with two cards from the pack in your hand.

3. The aim is to use all the cards in the pack, and get all the pairs together.

4. If you manage to do that, you win. Otherwise, shuffle the pack and start again.

TIP! Like all games of Patience, it is not as easy to get out as you think. Keep trying!

PaTience

This is the ultimate card game for one person. It's harder than the forms of Patience we've shown you earlier in the book, but it's so much fun that you'll keep coming back for more.

1. Remove the Jokers from a pack of cards and shuffle the pack well.

2. Deal seven cards in a row, in front of you. Lay them out so that the first card is facing up, and the remaining six are facing down.

3. Go back and deal over the top of these. But ignore the first card. Go to the second card and lay a card, face-up, on it. Continue to deal over the remaining five cards, face-down.

4. Deal again, starting on the third pile, face-up, then the rest face-down. Then deal again, starting with the fourth card, then the fifth, and so on, until you finally place a single face-up card on the seventh pile.

5. The rest of the pack is the stock. Place it in front, to your left, face-down.

6. The idea is to end up with four piles of cards – each of the suits face-up, with the Ace on the bottom, followed by the Two, the Three, etc., with the King on top.

7. Look at your seven piles of cards and look for ways of building runs of alternate colors on them. For example, if you have an Eight of Hearts on one pile and a Seven of Spades on the other, shift the Seven of Spades across to it, overlapping so you can see both.

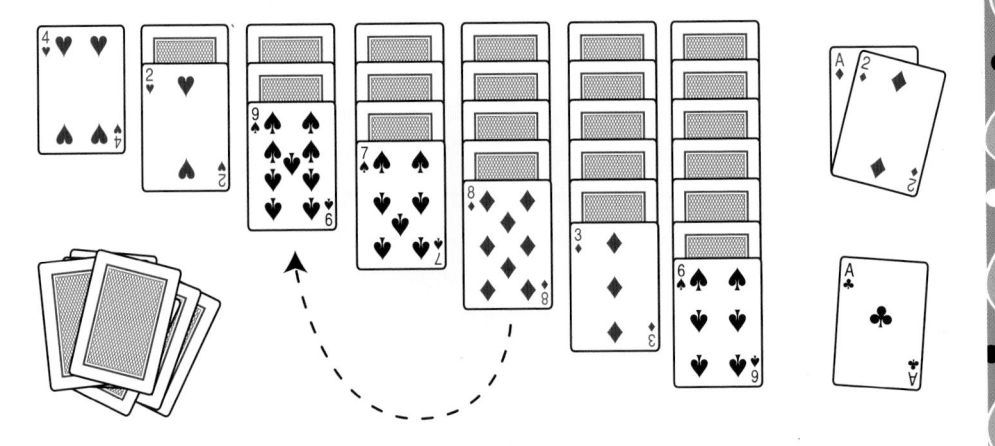

8. Each time you take a face-up card and move it, turn up the face-down card underneath it, and sit it face-up on top of the pile. Look around to see if it can be moved to another pile. You can then turn over the next card, and so on.

9. When you turn up an Ace, start a separate pile for it at the side.

10. Having put as many color cards in order as you can, turn to your stock pile. Holding it face-down, count three cards and then turn them up so you can see what the third card is. See if you can place it. If you can, look at the next card, and see if you can place it.

11. If you can't place any, put any remaining cards face-up on a pile to your right, and go to the next three. Keep working through the stock until it is finished. Don't worry if at any time you come down to just one or two cards at the end, instead of three. Use them as if they were three. Then turn the pile over and start again.

12. You will often come across two groups of cards that can be made into one. For example, one group might have a Red Eight at the bottom. Another has a Black Seven at the top, so you can shift it across. You must move all the cards.

13. If a pile disappears and becomes a space, you can put a King only in that space, and then start adding the Queen, Jack, Ten, etc.

14. Keep picking up cards in threes from your stock pile and using them where possible, shifting cards in colored sequence amongst the dealt piles, and building the suits on Aces.

15. If you reach a point where you simply cannot find a move, then that's it, you have not got Patience out. Shuffle the cards and start again. But with a bit of luck and some good playing, you will build up the Aces pile until everything is gone. You've been patient and got Patience out!

TIP! Never give up until you are certain you cannot make a move. It's amazing how, after going back over things, you'll find a move you missed.

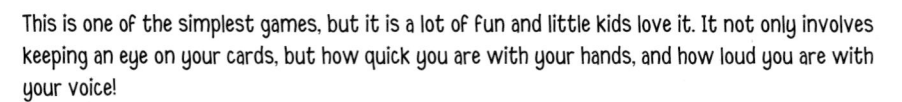 

Snap

This is one of the simplest games, but it is a lot of fun and little kids love it. It not only involves keeping an eye on your cards, but how quick you are with your hands, and how loud you are with your voice!

1. You can use one pack of cards, or two shuffled together if you like. Two people can play this, or as many as you like.

2. Deal all the cards out, so everyone has an equal amount.

3. The first player turns up a card. Then the second player turns up a card.

4. The idea is to look out for matching cards in a row. For example, two Threes or a pair of Kings.

5. If the cards do not match, then the next player puts a card down. But if the cards match, the players shout, "SNAP!"

6. The first player to shout, "SNAP!" takes the pile of cards.

7. If you like, you not only have to shout, "SNAP!", but put a hand on the cards, too. The first person to place his/her hands on the pile while saying, "SNAP!" gets the cards.

8. Keep going until one person gets all the cards and is the winner. Then start again!

TIP! It's all in the anticipation - try and read the players' faces, and watch every card as it is about to be put down.

SpiT

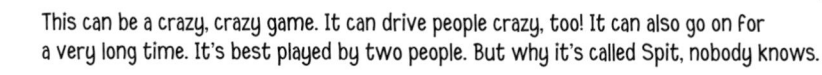

This can be a crazy, crazy game. It can drive people crazy, too! It can also go on for a very long time. It's best played by two people. But why it's called Spit, nobody knows.

1. Take out the Jokers from a pack of cards, shuffle well and deal the cards evenly between two players.

2. Each player deals out a series of cards in front of him/her, in similar form to Patience, but with only five piles. That is, deal one card face-up, then four cards face-down. Then ignore the first card and put one card face-up on the second pile, and a face-down card on each of the remaining three piles. Then ignore the first two piles and deal a card face-up on the third, and so on.

3. Each player puts his/her remaining cards in a pile, in the middle of the table. One pile for each player, facing each other, with a gap in between.

4. Each player checks along his/her face-up cards, to see if there are any pairs. For example, if you have two Threes, shift one Three across and put it on top of the other, and then turn over the top card of the remaining pile from where you took the Three. If you find another Three, put it with the other two. Keep shifting until all matches are made, and all piles have a face-up card on top.

5. Now the game begins, starting with the two piles you made in the middle. At a signal, both players turn the top card up from their own pile in the middle, and place it face-up on the table. These two cards will be the basis of all that follows.

6. Both players look at the two face-up cards in the middle of the table, and see if they can place some of their cards on either one, either higher or lower. For example, if one of the cards is a Four, then you can either put a Three on it, or a Five. Say you put a Three on it, then now you have the option of putting a Two on it, or a Four. The thing is, so does your opponent. Get it down quick!

7. To make the game even more interesting, the rule is that you can only use one hand!

8. Each time you take a face-up card from the cards in front of you and place it on either of the middle piles, you then turn over the face-down card underneath. If it is in a sequence, you continue on, and put it in the middle. If it is a pair with one of your other cards, put it with that, and turn over the next card on the pile.

9. If a space appears in front of you, place one of your face-up cards there, too. This gives you the chance to turn over another one of your face-down cards.

10. Every now and then, you will come to a halt and nothing will run in sequence for either of you. So, at the agreed signal, you turn over the top two cards on the piles in the middle, and start again.

11. At some point, one player will run out of cards in front of him/her. This player then puts a hand on the smaller of the two face-up piles in the middle, just like Snap. The other player has to take the other, larger pile of face-up cards. Each player also takes back his/her pile of face-down cards from the middle.

12. You then deal the cards out in front of you, as you did at the beginning of the game, and start again

13. The game is won when a player goes to deal the cards out in front of him/her, but cannot make the beginnings of five piles – that is, he/she has four cards or less. At last, a winner has been found!

14. Finally, if you are game enough, shuffle the cards thoroughly, deal them, and start all over again.

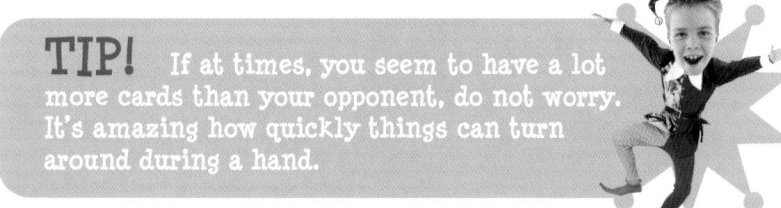

TIP! If at times, you seem to have a lot more cards than your opponent, do not worry. It's amazing how quickly things can turn around during a hand.

Whist

This is the simplest, basic version of a group of games that includes Euchre, Five Hundred, Solo and Contract Bridge. It's probably the hardest game in this book, but if you can learn this, you are well on the way to learning other games that will bring you a lifetime of enjoyment with friends and family.

Some Basic Ground Rules

Whist is a game for four players.

- The players pair off into two teams of two, and the team members always sit opposite each other.
- The idea is to win as many "tricks" as possible. You win a trick when you win a round in the game, just like German Whist, featured earlier in this book. If you win seven rounds, you have won seven tricks.
- Winning tricks hinge on what is "trumps". As in German whist, trumps are the leading suit of cards. A trump card always beats other cards. For example, if Clubs are trumps, the Three of Clubs will beat the King of Diamonds. The only card that can beat a trump card is another, higher trump card. When clubs are trumps, the highest value card in the game is the Ace of Clubs.
- In each suit, the highest value card is Ace, followed by King, Queen etc. down to Two.

How To Get Started

1. Decide who will deal the first hand. Cut the pack, as shown in German Whist, with the person who selects the lowest card earning the right to deal. (In cutting the deal for process only, the Ace is regarded as the lowest card.)

2. The dealer discards the two Jokers and deals the remaining fifty-two cards, one at a time, clockwise, starting with the player on his/her left, until each person has thirteen cards.

3. When all cards are dealt, which suit will be the trump suit is decided by turning up, or showing, the last card dealt. Say, for example, the Eight of Diamonds is turned up. Then, Diamonds is trumps.

4. All players take their thirteen cards and fan them out, facing inwards, so no one else can see them.

PLay GeTs Underway

1. The player to the left of the dealer plays first, or leads, by putting one card down in front, face-up, so all can see.

2. Play always goes clockwise, with the second, third and fourth players now putting a card down.

3. Players must follow the suit of the first card. If it is a Club, for example, you must play a Club.

4. If you cannot follow suit, you have two choices – either put a card of another suit down, or play a trump card.

5. The person with the strongest card – either the highest of the lead suit cards or the highest trump card, wins the trick.

6. The winner collects the four cards and puts them in a neat pile, face-down, to one side. This is called a trick.

7. The winner of the trick also gets to lead for the next round.

8. And so the game goes on, until all cards are gone and thirteen tricks have been won.

TIP! Try to remember which cards have been played. By watching closely, try to guess what cards your partner may have. Then lead, so that he/she may win those tricks.

Trumps

- A trump card may only be played if trumps are lead, or if the player has none of the suit that has been lead in his/her hand.
- The highest trump card always wins the trick.
- Failure to follow suit when possible is called reneging. It is illegal, and incurs a penalty of three tricks.

The Team

- Don't forget you are working with the person opposite you, and the object is to win the game together. Do not trump your partner's winning trick.
- You have to watch the cards, and try to work out what your partner has.
- You will get good at "feeding" your partner a low card of a certain suit, so he/she can play a high card of that suit, and you win the trick. And vice versa.

Scoring

- You will need a sheet of paper and a pen to keep the score.
- It is possible to win thirteen tricks. After a team as won six tricks, any tricks after that are scoring tricks. They score one point per trick.
- To score, subtract 6 from the number of tricks you have taken. For example, if you have taken nine tricks, 9 – 6 = 3, therefore, your score for that round = 3.
- After the score is tallied, you are ready for the next round. The dealer is now the player on the left of the person who dealt last.
- Scoring styles in Whist vary, but before the game starts set a target, and the first team to reach it is the winner.
- Alternatively, you might set a time limit and the team in front at that point is the winner.

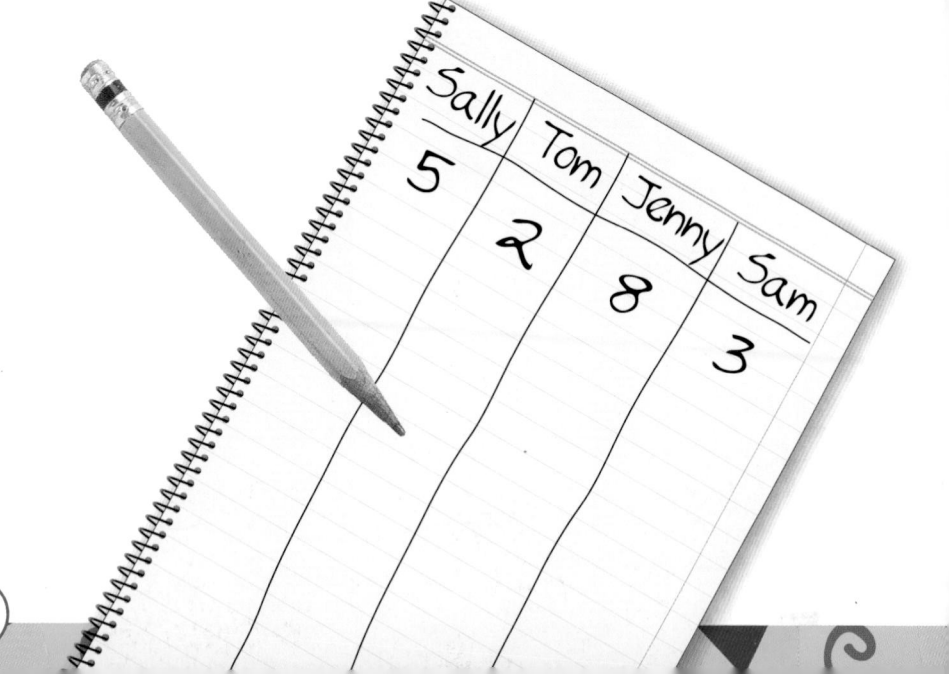

CARD TRICKS

Card tricks are important part of every magician's act. But anyone can have fun with them. The card tricks in the following pages are some of the best around. Give them a try!

Before You Begin

We all know somebody who owns a pack of cards and loves to bore everyone with poorly rehearsed card tricks. Don't be like that. Become good at your tricks so people enjoy seeing you perform!

Here are The Three Ps of card Tricks:

Practice Your Tricks

You will not become a good card magician overnight. Magic is an art and takes many years to learn! Start with just one trick and learn one trick at a time. Carry your cards in your pocket, and at every opportunity, practice tricks on your friends and family.

Practice Your Patter

The words you say and the jokes you make when you do your card tricks not only entertain, but also distract the audience from what you're doing. When the audience is being entertained, you can get away with many things. If they are bored, they will be watching you closely and waiting for you to make a mistake. Your patter needs to be good.

Practice Your Look

Will you perform your tricks before an audience? Or will you simply carry a pack of cards in your pocket and entertain only one or two people at a time? Either way, you need to decide what sort of look you are going to have. You could wear a costume, with top hat, tails and a coat, like a traditional magician. Or you could dress as a clown, with a red nose and brightly colored clothes. One thing is for certain, whatever you wear, you need to have big pockets and plenty of them. Dress like a magician and you are well on your way to being one!

Now Let's get down to those card Tricks.

A Simple Card Trick

When you first begin to do card tricks, it's best to start off simple, to get the hang of things. The following simple trick relies on the fact that you know which card is on the bottom of the pack. Many cards tricks are based on this one, so if you master it, you are well on the way to becoming a good card magician.

It's important that you shuffle the pack well in order for this trick to work, so spend some time practicing your shuffling beforehand. A good thing to do if you are serious about shuffling well, is to always have a pack of cards in your pocket. Then, if you have a spare moment, you can get a couple of shuffles in.

This Is How You Do It

1. Take a pack of cards and fan them out.

2. Ask a friend to select one, look at it, remember what it is and give it back to you, without telling you what it is.

3. Return the card to the pack without looking at it.

4. Shuffle the pack.

5. Go through the cards and pick out the one he/she selected. Say, "This is your card!"

How Did You Do That?

- Before you begin, look at the card that is on the bottom of the pack and remember it. (Let's say it is the Six of Diamonds.)
- When your friend hands you back the card, simply put it at the bottom, underneath the Six of Diamonds, and start shuffling.
- The key is to make it look like you are shuffling really well – but not to shuffle too hard!
- The idea is that during the shuffle, the Six of Diamonds and the mystery card will stay together.
- Practice on your own, you will get the hang of it. The more theatrical you are, the better the impact.
- Then turn the cards to you, fan them out, and look through them. The card on the right of the Six of Diamonds will be the mystery card.

Behind The Back

This trick is called a "key card" trick. A key card is a card that has been altered in some way, so it is apparent to the magician where it sits in the pack. Key card tricks are some of the best around – you can astound your audience with your ability to apparently remember, or mentally work out, what a particular card is.

In this trick, you are able to locate a given card, while you are holding the pack behind your back. Because you bend the remainder of the cards while the volunteer is looking at the chosen card, that card will be the only flat card when it is returned to the pack, and so, the pack will be split there. The one flat card is your key card!

This Is How You Do It

1. Spread the pack face-down, along a table.

2. Choose a volunteer and ask him/her to choose a card.

3. As the volunteer looks at the card he/she has chosen, close the pack together, pick up the cards, and buckle them in your hand.

4. Spread the cards on the table.

5. Ask the volunteer to return his/her card to anywhere in the pack.

6. Take the cards, square them, and hand them to the volunteer to be shuffled.

7. As the chosen card is the only flat card in the pack, it will show a distinct split where it has been inserted.

8. Take the cards and square them again. While you are doing this, make sure that the chosen card is near the center of the pack. You may have to shuffle it there. If it is centered, don't shuffle.

9. Place the pack behind your back, telling the audience that you have power in your fingers, and that they will locate the chosen card.

10. Once the cards are behind your back, you will be able to locate the chosen card by holding the cards lightly. They will divide where the flat card is located.

11. Gently cut (separate) the cards at the divide. The chosen card will be the bottom card of the cut.

12. Slide the chosen card into your right hand – the others will be in your left hand.

13. Place the pack on the table.

14. Place the chosen card on top of it, and enjoy the amazement on the faces of your audience!

TIP! Keep that patter up! Chat to your audience, talking smoothly to them about the power in your fingers, while you have your hands behind your back and are sorting the chosen card from the pack.

Dip and Deal

This card trick is called an "illusion". A good magician is a master of illusion. He or she is able to make it look as though things are happening, when in fact, they are not!

In this trick, you mix up the cards according to the instructions that you have been given by a member of the audience. However, they always end up in the same way that they began.

You must employ a lot of clever patter when doing this trick, to disguise the fact that you are not really doing anything. Therefore, the better the patter, the more effective the trick.

This Is How You Do It

1. Take all thirteen cards of one suit and lay them in numerical order, on a table.
Ask your audience to take particular note of the strict order of the cards.

2. Square up the pile, so it is nice and neat.

3. Turn the pile face-down in your left hand.

4. Explain to your audience that you want to make sure that the cards are thoroughly mixed up, and ask somebody to oversee the task and help you do it.

5. Explain to your new assistant that when he/she tells you to "deal", you will put a card on the table.

6. When the assistant says "dip", you will take a second card from the pile, and place it on top of the first card.

7. Deal both cards together on the table.

8. Follow the assistant's instructions, and "dip" or "deal" all of the thirteen cards.

9. Pick up the pile and square it again.

10. Now say, "That has mixed the cards up, but just to be sure, let's do it again."

11. Repeat the process, either "dipping" or "dealing" as instructed.

12. Pick up the pile, square it again and say, "The thing is that these cards have a mind of their own, and always go back to where they were in the beginning."

13. Turn the cards over and spread them.

14. All the cards will be back in numerical order.

How Did You Do That?

- When you place the second card on top of the first one, you reverse the order of the cards.
- When you repeat the process the second time, you are again reversing the order back to where you began.

Guiding Hand

Here is another trick that relies on the magician knowing the location of a "key card".
This time, the key card has been marked with a pencil-mark that only the magician can see. The chosen card is dropped on top of or beneath it, so that it is easy to find. A volunteer is required to guide the magician's finger, in order to locate his/her card.

This Is How You Do It

1. Make a key card by taking a card from the pack, and marking it with a pencil dot on the top right and bottom left hand corner.

2. Return the marked card to the top of the pack.

3. Ask a volunteer from the audience to step forward, and help you.

4. Cut (separate) the pack, taking the top pile in your right hand and offering the top of the bottom pile to the volunteer.

cutting the pack

5. Ask the volunteer to pick a card, any card.

40

6. Return the right hand pile to the left, dropping the marked card onto the top of the left pile, and so on top of the chosen card.

7. Shuffle the cards.

8. Cut the cards a couple of times and then spread them over the table, taking note of the position of the marked card.

9. Ask the volunteer to go looking with you. Offer him/her your hand, and point your finger. Instruct him/her to hold your wrist, so that together you will find the mystery card.

10. Practice what you are going to say, and be sure to play up the "guided hand" angle, making the audience believes that you have no say in where your finger will land.

11. When you come close to the marked card, begin to lower your hand slowly, so that it is not obvious to the audience.

12. Let your finger come to rest on the card to the left of the marked card, and you will have located the chosen card!

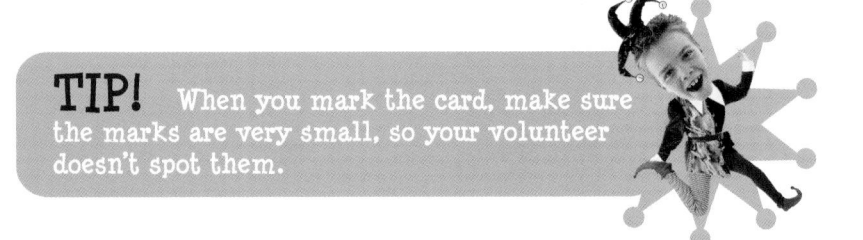

TIP! When you mark the card, make sure the marks are very small, so your volunteer doesn't spot them.

Secret Messages

Here is another great trick that uses a "key card" with a message that you will make up beforehand. The message will say, "You have run out of cards." It is important that you are very accurate in your placing of the card in the pack, and with your counting, too. You must also be entertaining with your patter, to make this trick enjoyable for your audience.

This Is How You Do It

1. Make a message card by sticking a label across the face of one of the cards in the pack.

2. Place this card in the twenty-first position from the top of the pack.

3. Lay the pack on the table.

4. Ask a volunteer to take some cards from the top of the pack and put them in his/her pocket. Say something like, "Not too many, though, or we will be here all day." This will ensure that he/she takes less than twenty-one cards.

5. Then say, "Now I will take some too."

6. You take twenty-one cards. Do not make it obvious that you are counting. Do this by picking up the pack and dealing twenty-one cards onto the table.

7. Put the pack aside and pick up your twenty-one cards.

8. "Okay," you say, "now we will take turns to deal cards onto the table. I will go first."

9. You deal a card onto the table, turning it face-up.

10. The volunteer takes one from his/her pocket and places it face-up on the table.

11. Continue doing this until you deal the message card.

12. The volunteer reaches into his/her pocket and discovers that all his/her cards are gone.

13. Now that's magic!

How Did You Do That?

The volunteer takes their cards from the top of the pack and has been asked not to take too many, so we know that they will not take the message card. If they take fifteen cards, the message card will be six cards down. When you take exactly twenty-one cards and reverse the order of the cards, the message card will be at position fifteen in your hand, which is exactly when the volunteer will find that they have no cards left in their pocket!

The Three Column Trick

This trick relies on mathematics, and counting the cards. The best way to do card tricks that involve mathematics – especially if you do not trust your math skills – is to get the audience to help you! You also need to be able to convince the audience that you are having trouble finding the chosen card, and then actually finding the card. So practice your patter skills beforehand and keep them talking!

This Is How You Do It

1. Deal out three columns of seven cards, dealing from left to right, and face-up. Put the rest of the cards aside.

2. Ask for a volunteer and ask him/her to choose a card and remember it, without touching it. You will guess which card it is.

3. Tell him/her you seem to be having trouble getting the vibes, and have him/her point to the column that has the card.

4. Pick up all three columns in the following way:

5. Stack the column with the chosen card on top of the first column, but under the third.

6. Deal three columns again, exactly as before.

7. Frown, and pretend to be still searching for the column.

8. Ask the volunteer to tell you which column the card is in.

9. Pick the cards up in the same way as before – the column containing the card is in the middle.

10. Deal the columns again.

11. Tell the audience you will try once more.

12. Begin to deal the cards as before. This time, however, silently count to yourself until you reach the number 11.

13. Stop and look very relieved.

14. Hold up the card and say something like, "This is what I'm looking for."
    You've found the chosen card!

TIP! It's very important that you count the cards exactly when performing this trick. Practice, practice, practice, before you do it in front of an audience.

Unbelievable

Here is another card trick that involves mathematics and memory. Your audience will be convinced you have special powers if you get this one right!

This Is How You Do It

1. Memorize the tenth card in the pack.

2. Ask for a volunteer and give him/her the pack of cards. Ask them to think of a number between ten and twenty, and to deal that number of cards, face-down, into a pile on the table.

3. Put the rest of the pack aside.

4. Ask the volunteer to add together the digits of his/her number. For example, if the number was 15, then 1+5=6.

5. Using the cards already dealt, square the pack and hand to the volunteer, and ask if he/she would now deal out that number of cards.

6. This card will always be the tenth card, which you have memorized.

7. Ask your volunteer to look at his/her card.

8. You will now tell the audience which card your volunteer is holding. Unbelievable!

TIP! There are several ways that you can reveal the card the volunteer is holding. You can ask him/her to look at the card, and then "read their mind" by predicting which one it is. You can reshuffle the pack and deal the cards, announcing the card when it appears. Or you may wish to devise your own theatrical method.

Upside Down

Here is another trick that relies on illusion. You need to be able to keep attention away from the card at the bottom of the pack, which is the only card turned the wrong way. Keep it tucked firmly in behind the second bottom card on the pack, so that no one but you knows that it is there. You also need a wand for this trick. You could make one from a piece of thin, round wood, or a long pencil.

This Is How You Do It

1. Turn over the bottom card of the pack and place the rest of the pack right way up, on top of it.

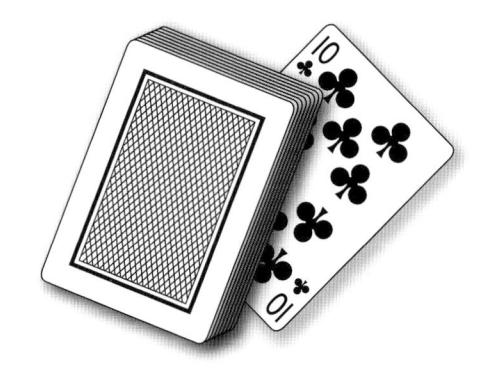

2. Spread the cards face-down on a table, being careful not to show the bottom card. Then ask a volunteer to choose a card.

3. Tell him/her to show the card to the audience, but not to show it to you.

4. While the volunteer is showing the card, close the pack and turn it over, so that the bottom card is on top and it appears as if all of the pack is face-down.

5. Ask the volunteer to place the card back into the pack, face-down and anywhere he/she likes.

6. Tell the volunteer that he/she is about to perform some magic, and hand him/her your wand.

7. Turn over the hand holding the pack, so your hand is now palm-down, and put the pack of cards on the table. Be sure to keep that bottom card tucked in, so it cannot be seen. The cards are now right side up.

8. Ask your volunteer to tap the cards with the magic wand, and tell him/her to say some magic words

9. Pick up the pack, and fan the cards out on the table, once again keeping the bottom card hidden.

10. The selected card will be easy to spot – it will be the only card upside down!

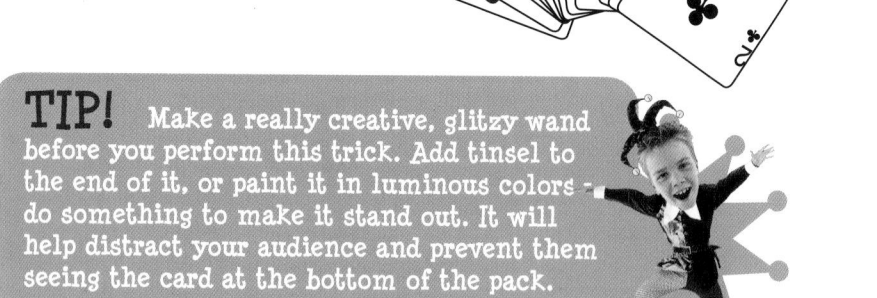

TIP! Make a really creative, glitzy wand before you perform this trick. Add tinsel to the end of it, or paint it in luminous colors – do something to make it stand out. It will help distract your audience and prevent them seeing the card at the bottom of the pack.

DICE GAMES

Dice games are some of the oldest games in history. Dice have even been found in ancient Egyptian tombs! It's no wonder dice games have been played for thousands of years – they're so much fun! We've featured some of the best in the following pages of this book.

10 Things You Should Know About Dice

1. A single dice is called a die.

2. Dice is the plural form of the word, and refers to more than one die.

3. All dice (except some novelty dice) are six sided cubes.

4. Each die is numbered 1 to 6.

5. The numbers on a die are generally shown as spots (also known as "pips") on the surface of the cube.

6. The standard size of a die is $^{3}/_{4}$ inch (18mm).

7 The numbers on a die are always arranged so that any two opposing sides add up to 7.

8. Most modern dice are made of plastic. Dice used in casinos are made to very precise standards, to eliminate the risk of them landing one particular way all the time.

9. Different dice games use different numbers of dice. Most games use from two to five dice.

10. Dice games are purely games of chance, or luck. There is no way to control how the dice fall when they are thrown. That's what makes a game of dice so exciting!

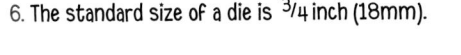

Aces in The Pot

This fun and simple game can be enjoyed by two or more players of all ages. You'll need two dice and some counters to get the game rolling.

1. Each player takes two counters and then takes it in turn to roll one die.

2. The player with the highest number goes first, and then play moves clockwise around the table.

3. If a player throws an Ace (a "1") they put one counter in the pot (or kitty), in the centre of the table. If two Aces are thrown, both counters go into the pot and the player is out of that round.

4. If a player throws a 6, they give a counter to the player on their left. If a player throws two 6s, both counters are given to the player on their left. All other throws do not count.

5. Only players who have counters can continue to throw the dice.

6. When the dice come to the last player to hold a counter, they are thrown three times. If there is no 6 in those three throws, the player wins the pot.

7. If a 6 is thrown by the last player, the last counter and the dice are passed to the player on the left. The first player to throw the dice three times without throwing a 6 wins the pot.

8. In the next round of the game, everyone is given two more counters, and the person to the left of the first player in the last round begins again.

TIP! The more players that join in this game, the more fun it is. This makes it a very good game to play at family get-togethers!

BeeTLe

This is a good first dice game for the youngest of players. Two to six people can play, and players can also be arranged in teams. You'll need a single die and some pencils and paper, too.

1. The aim of this game is to try to throw the scores that will allow you or your team to be the first to draw a complete beetle. Each beetle must have thirteen parts – one head, two antennae, two eyes, a body, six legs and a tail.

2. The scores for Beetle are:
   1 – draw the body
   2 – draw the head
   3 – draw a leg
   4 – draw an eye
   5 – draw an antenna
   6 – draw a tail

3. The youngest player starts the game, then the person to the left of that player takes a turn, and so on.

4. Depending on their score, the player may be able to draw in part of their (or their team's) beetle.

5. But – before starting to draw, the player must throw a 1, as the body part must be the first part drawn.

6. Other parts can then be added to the beetle, according to the number thrown.

7. The winner is the first player, or team, to complete a beetle.

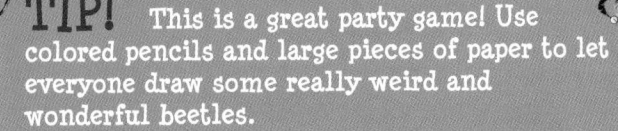

TIP! This is a great party game! Use colored pencils and large pieces of paper to let everyone draw some really weird and wonderful beetles.

Centennial

Get a group of friends together for this game. Two to eight people can play. You'll need three dice, a board or piece of paper marked with a row of boxes numbered 1 to 12, and one different colored counter for each player.

1. The object of Centennial is to be the first player to move their counter from Box 1 to Box 12 and back again, according to the throw of the dice.

2. To begin, players roll one die to see who will be the first shooter (a shooter is the person who throws the dice). The player with the highest score goes first.

3. Each player in turn throws the three dice once. Their throw must contain a 1 before they can begin to play. If they do not throw a 1, they must pass the dice to the next player.

4. When a player has thrown a 1, they place their counter on the box numbered 1. Now they must try to throw a 2, so they can move to Box 2, and so on. If they do not throw a 2, they must once again pass the dice to the next player.

5. Just to make things a little easier, the number a player needs to throw can be made up with all three dice. For instance, a 2 can be made up by throwing a 1, 1 and a 6 (the six wouldn't count).

6. If a player is lucky enough to throw a 1, 2, 3, they can move through Boxes 1, 2 and 3 right away, but also through Box 4 (1+3), Box 5 (3+2) and even Box 6 (1+2+3)!

7. Here's another interesting rule - if a player throws a required number but overlooks it, that number can be claimed by any other player who needs it, and can use it immediately.

8. The first player to finish the journey from 1 to 12 and back again to 1, is the winner.

TIP Be sure to keep a close eye on your opponents when playing Centennial. If they overlook a number they could use (which is really easy to do), it will be to your advantage if you spot it first and get the chance to use it to move your own counter forward.

YOU WIN

Hint You can bet candy on this exciting game, too. Give each person a small amount of candy before play begins. Then each of you place some candy into the kitty (the kitty is the combined stakes of money, candy, or whatever players are betting with. The kitty may also be called the pot). The winner collects the kitty at the end of the game!

Craps

Craps is the most well-known dice game in the world and is played at casinos everywhere. It is also the biggest gambling game in the U. S. A. However, Craps is also a great game for all the family to play at home. You can use counters to place bets with, although candy is much more fun!

1. Craps is a game for two or more players. You'll need two dice, counters or pieces of candy, and a flat surface on which to play, such as a floor or large table.

2. First, players decide what the maximum bet will be (say ten counters). The first player, known as the shooter, announces the amount he or she will bet and places the counters in the center pot (also called kitty), saying, "I'll shoot five", or whatever amount they wish to bet. This means they are betting five counters to win.

3. Now the other players can "fade", or bet against the shooter by covering that player's bet and putting their money in the center pot. One player can cover the whole bet or several players can cover parts of it, say by five players all putting in one counter.

4. Any part of the shooter's stake that is not covered must be withdrawn before the dice are rolled. Players do not have to bet every time.

5. When the shooter's bet has been covered or faded, that player takes up the dice and throws them. Both dice have to be able to be seen by all those betting and if one dice has landed in such a way that it is doubtful which side is showing, the throw must be repeated.

6. If the first roll of the dice adds up to a 7 or 11 (a natural), the shooter wins.
   If it adds up to a 2, 3 or 12 (known as craps), the shooter loses.

7. If the shooter's roll adds up to 4, 5, 6, 8, 9 or 10, that number becomes the shooter's "point". This means they have to roll the dice again and again until the same number is rolled.

8. If the shooter rolls a 7 before they make a point, the bet is lost and the dice are passed to the player on the left.

9. Between rolls, the shooter can voluntarily pass on the dice at any time.

10. If the shooter wins, they get to take all the counters in the pot. If the shooter loses, those players who faded each take double the amount of counters they put in – so they get back their original bet, plus their share of the shooter's stake. So, if the shooter bets five counters and five separate players faded one counter each, when the shooter loses, each of the betting players receives two counters back and the shooter loses all five.

11. Players can also bet among themselves as to whether the player will win or lose. Players can also bet separately with the shooter. This is called side-betting.

Total possible combinations	Number of ways	Odds Against
2	1	35-1
3	2	17-1
4	3	11-1
5	4	8-1
6	5	31-5
7	6	5-1
8	5	31-5
9	4	8-1
10	3	11-1
11	2	17-1
12	1	35-1

TIP! Remember, Craps is a game of chance so you never know which numbers you are going to throw. That's one of the things that makes this game so exciting. However, some combinations of numbers come up more often than others. Take a look at the chart below to see which combinations of numbers you're more likely to throw.

Drop Dead

You will need five dice and a paper and pencil to play this exciting game for two or more players. Drop dead can be played as a gambling game, so get out the candy or counters and make a bet! Each player puts an agreed number of counters into the kitty before the first shooter rolls.

1. The aim of this game is to make the highest total score. Use the pencil and paper to keep track of each player's score.

2. First, each player throws a single die to decide the order of play. The player who throws the lowest number on the die goes first. Then the person to the left of that player takes a turn, and so on.

3. The first player throws all five dice. If any 2s or 5s are thrown, then nothing is scored

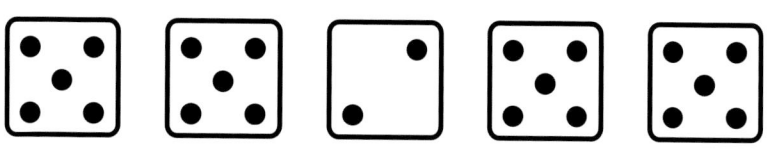

4. The player must take out any dice showing 2s or 5s and they are declared "dead".

5. If no 2s or 5s appear, the total score on the dice is added up and written down.

6. Now the player takes another turn, throwing the remainder of the dice and repeating steps 4 and 5.

7. The first player continues until all the dice have been eliminated. Then the player is said to have "dropped dead"!

8. Now play moves to the next player and continues around, until everyone has had a turn.

9. At the end of the round, the scores for each player are tallied and the player with the highest score is the winner.

TIP! This game can also be played with each player having just one throw per turn with one die only, and passing it on to the player on the left after each throw. Scores are tallied on a score card or piece of paper, to include the actual running total as well as how many dice the player has left.

Hearts or Hearts Due

You will need six dice and a pencil and paper, to get started.
Special dice marked with the letters HEARTS instead of numbers can be used in this game. However, it is easy to play with numbered dice, too. Just substitute the numbers for the letters, so that H=1, E=2, A=3, R=4, T=5 and S=6.

1. Players can either agree that the winner is the person to score more than the others over a decided number of rounds, or in a single round, or up to an agreed total, say, 150.

2. A throw of one die per player decides who is to throw first. The highest scorer usually has the honor. Each player in turn rolls the six dice once, and calculates their score according to the following:

1 (H)	5 pts
1, 2 (HE)	10 pts
1, 2, 3, (HEA)	15 pts
1, 2, 3, 4, (HEAR)	20pts
1, 2, 3, 4, 5, (HEART)	25 pts
1, 2, 3, 4, 5, 6, (HEARTS)	35 pts

3. If a double (such as two 4s) or a treble (such as three 5s) is scored when the six dice are thrown, only one of them counts. However, if three 1s appear, the player's whole score is wiped out, and they have to begin again!

TIP! You can buy lots of different types of dice from most toy and game stores.

Help Your Neighbor

This is a fast, fun and furious game that everyone loves! You can win or lose a fortune (of counters) in an hour or so! Two to six people can play - you'll need ten counters for each player and three dice.

1. Each player is given ten counters to begin.

2. If there are six players, each person chooses a number from 1 to 6; if there are five playing, players take numbers from 1 to 5 and 6 is not in play, and is ignored when it comes up in a throw. With four players, both the 5 and 6 are ignored, but with three players, each takes two numbers. If only two are playing, each takes three numbers.

3. Play moves clockwise around the table, beginning with the player who is number 1.

4. Each player throws the three dice and when a player's number comes up they must put a counter in the pot (kitty), one for each number. So, if there are six players and one throw sees 6, 4, 2 come up, those players put in one counter each. However, if there is a throw which has 3, 3, 5, the player who is number three has to put in two counters.

5. The first player to run out of counters wins the round! The next round will begin with the player who is number 2.

TIP! This is another great game where candy can be used instead of counters. Winning the pot is much more fun if you get to eat it afterwards!

Indian Dice

This game for two or more players is similar to another game, called Poker Dice.
Poker Dice is usually played with specially marked dice but with Indian Dice, all you need are five ordinary dice to start having fun!

1. The aim of Indian Dice is to score the highest possible poker hand (poker is a popular card game), using the dice.

2. The poker hands rank as follows:
   Five of a kind – highest
   Four of a kind
   Full house
   Three of a kind
   Two pairs
   Pair
   No pair

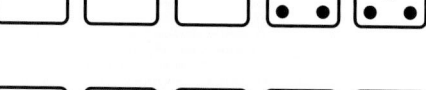

3. Each player rolls one die, to see who plays, or shoots, first. The highest scorer becomes the shooter, and then has up to three throws to set up a hand.

4. The shooter can "stand" (miss a turn) on their first throw if they think they have a good score, or pick up any or all of the dice for a second throw. Again, they may stand on that throw or pick up any or all of the dice for a third and final throw.

5. None of the following players can make any more throws than the first shooter.

6. The game usually involves two rounds, with the winners of each round playing for any stakes (counters or candy), if they are involved.

7. If no stakes are involved, often the lowest scorers play off for a win. If there are only two players, the winner is the one who wins two out of three rounds.

TIP! You can vary this game by making the Ace (one spot), or any other number "wild". This means the Ace or the number you choose can be any value you want it to be.

Thirty-six

This simple family dice game is loads of fun and can be played by two or more players. You'll need one die, a pencil and paper for scoring, and some counters for the pot (kitty).

1. The object of Thirty-six is for players to score a total of 36 points. However, any player who scores more than 36 points is out of the game!

2. The winner is often the player whose score is nearest to 36 points. That player usually takes the pot.

3. Each player puts an agreed amount of counters into the pot; say five each for four players.

4. Then each player rolls the die. The player with the highest number goes first, then the next highest number, and so on.

5. Now the first player rolls the die once. That player keeps note of the score and passes the die to the next player, who does the same thing.

6. Play continues around the table, round by round.

7. As a player nears 36, they may choose to miss a turn or "stand" on their score. In this way, they hope they will not go over 36 and be out of the game.

8. The first person to reach 36 or get closest to 36, or the last person left in the game is the winner.

9. In the event of a tie, the pot is usually divided.

TIP! Keep an eye on your score, as you get close to 36. If you have 30, you will not be able to throw more than 6 and go out of the game. But if you have 33 or higher, it may be best to "stand", or miss a turn.

Yacht

Yacht is known as a "category game" among dice games. Many people will know it as Yahtzee®, which is its commercial form. It is similar to the game General, a favorite game in Puerto Rico. Any number of players can play this game, but it's best for five or six. You will need five dice, and a paper and pencil for a score sheet.

1. Players throw one die to determine who goes first, with the lowest score beginning the game.

2. The first player then rolls the five dice, sets aside any dice they wish to keep, and throws for a second and third time, to try to improve their hand.

The following table shows the hands to aim for, and the scores they achieve.

HAND	POINTS
Yacht (five of a kind)	50
Big Straight (2, 3, 4, 5, 6)	30
Little Straight (1, 2, 3, 4, 5)	30
Four of a Kind	pip value
Full House (any three of a kind, and two of a kind)	pip value
Choice (any five dice of no specific pattern)	pip value
Sixes, fives, fours, threes, twos & aces (ones)	pip value for every dice thrown in each category

3. When the first player has thrown three times, they must then decide the category in which to place the total score.

4. Now it is the next player's turn. Play proceeds clockwise around the group.

5. Play in one game continues for twelve rounds, when each player must have entered a score for each category, even if that score is zero (this will often be the case). When a score is entered into a category, it stays, and cannot be superseded by a superior score in that same category later on.

6. Players add up their scores at the end of twelve rounds, and the highest total wins the game.

TIP! Try for large scores early on in this game. They may help you win in the end, when the scores are added up.

THE END